Black Dog Day

poems by

Brian Burt

Finishing Line Press
Georgetown, Kentucky

Black Dog Day

For Christina, Alex, and, of course, Milo

Copyright © 2022 by Brian Burt
ISBN 978-1-64662-895-7 First Edition
All rights reserved under International and Pan-American Copyright Conventions. No part of this book may be reproduced in any manner whatsoever without written permission from the publisher, except in the case of brief quotations embodied in critical articles and reviews.

Publisher: Leah Huete de Maines
Editor: Christen Kincaid
Cover Art: Brian Burt
Author Photo: C. Scherer
Cover Design: Elizabeth Maines McCleavy

Order online: www.finishinglinepress.com
also available on amazon.com

Author inquiries and mail orders:
Finishing Line Press
PO Box 1626
Georgetown, Kentucky 40324
USA

Table of Contents

Black Dog Day 1

On Being a Dog 2

All Bark 3

The Morning News 4

January Morning with Black Dog 5

Prayer that Begins in the Eye of a Dog 7

In a Time of Drought, Praise 9

The Heart of the Matter 11

Unsung Song 13

Police Log 14

Loyal Companions 17

The Beginning of the End of the Beginning 18

On the Morning of a Sudden Death 19

In This or Any Other World 20

Sowing Winter Rye 23

Puget Sound 24

Still Life, With Marriage 25

Notes 27

With Thanks 28

Dogs are minor angels.
—*Jonathan Carroll*

BLACK DOG DAY

Some mornings begin in such quiet—
gray and colorless, before the sun rises,
before most of the world shakes
its fur to greet the day—
that I feel as still and clear
as a cold glass of water
on a warm afternoon,
and even though I just woke
and came downstairs in the dark
and drank a hot cup of coffee with cream
and am now sitting here writing,
something like a heavy-lidded drowsiness
descends inside my head and my eyes relax
and my jaw begins to unclench.
I can then hear the sound of a door
being pushed open upstairs,
like the sound of a page
turning, like a distant low wave
falling into white foam on shore—
and as he does every morning
my black dog bounds
down the stairs
to stand before me
panting, eyes expectant,
waiting to be fed.

ON BEING A DOG
—after Ross Gay

Sliding hands along
his fur-slicked spine, feeling
slack skin slipping over bone
and then loosening the leash
and seeing shimmer of drool
smeared on pink tongue
remakes me to a blur
of black fur that gleams
and streaks across green grass,
coming back with dead sparrow
in my maw, teeth clamping
harder for a grip, dropping it
when commanded and then
touching nose-tip
to each blade of grass
to track new scent,
each eye still taking in
any shift of wing,
every twitch of grass.

Then, pressing my hand
to his paw makes me feel
a need in joint and jaw—
bark, whine, wag,
then silence and surge
with field underfoot in a sprint,
fur sheening, wet tongue
casting off every plan
but to run and run
and run and run
until paws pull up short
of chain-link fence,
pure present tense.

ALL BARK
    —*after lowellgm*

Words aren't dogs and so don't fetch
or heel or stretch in noonday sun.
Still, when packed together they'll spin out
prowling, pellucid thought, wanting to convince you
that they'll come running when called or will sink
their teeth into your enemy's leg or can sprint
across green grass between shadow and glint
of sun from you to the fence and back.
They're always hungry for more than they can tell.
But in themselves, no jaw, no snout, no tongue,
no eagerly thumping barbaric tail.

THE MORNING NEWS

Flake by flake snow fills the tracks
I left behind this morning
when I got the daily paper from the stoop.
Before morning coffee, I'm still tired and
unsure that I can loop through
more outraged babble, more
tweets taunting us to stick
our microscopes up our climatology
and get over it, more headlines
dive bombing their way
across the page into my morning air.

These calamities take me nowhere
I prefer to go, so I leave the house
to walk the dog and wander in the snow
beyond my neighbor's place, make my way
to Walden Woods, where blurred mist rises
off thin ice over Fairhaven Bay.
My black dog leads me
down the snow-packed path—

movement of gray air,
winter boots crunching
past a thing elusive as a scent
that only dogs can smell,
cheeks flushed red in the face of a wind
that no one will recall but me.
I thank the trees, I thank the air,
as I stare at a fading light brighter
in my eyes than the glow of burning books
in a distant city square at night.

JANUARY MORNING WITH BLACK DOG

1.
Ice, frozen sand, scraps of snow,
at water's edge by Fairhaven Bay,
mist in tatters rises—and
my dog and I circle the shore
where, nose to the ground,
he discovers a carcass
of some small mammal heaped
in a mound on the ice and sand,
bones and tufts of fur scattered
all around. He buries his snout
in the whole mess to find
what can't be found.

2.
Chalky scoured bones,
color of dirty snow,
rough circular symmetry,
signature of all things.
Delicate skeleton
unlocked from flesh, no
secret closets of a body here—
ribs and sloping snout,
empty orbits in the skull,
tarsus, metatarsus, tibia—
surfaces stripped clean
of meat by scavengers.

3.
A croak stammers across floes,
water flows beneath, and
then a high-pitched yowl pierces,
like a human infant in pain.
Coyote? Fisher-cat? I can't tell.

Bare branches quiver above shore
and another yowl echoes down to us.
My dog's soft ears prick up
stiff with unknown sound.

4.
All seems headed down its own path
and nothing here belongs to us—
inhuman cries beyond the trees,
sun disappearing, almost reappearing,
behind tattered gray January clouds,
half-moon hidden somewhere in our sky,
always there, always there, even when unseen—
curved paths of our spheres
promising nothing for now,
nothing but more cold and snow,
more ice, more bones,
vacuum of space, gravity always
holding our feet to a path,
as we try to avoid ice-slicked stones.

5.
The water of the bay groans
beneath its own frozen weight.
My dog's nose twitches,
as eyes scan the ragged tree-line
and his leash tugs my hand away
from where I want to go.
He wants to follow the scent
of whatever's watching our feet
scrawl their way across the snow.
I tug the leash back a bit too hard,
say *This way, buddy, this way,*
try to steer us back on track
to take the short loop home.

PRAYER THAT BEGINS IN THE EYE OF A DOG

Angels have never said a word to me.
No wings, no fulgent fingers pointing
to passages in illuminated manuscripts.
They've never instructed me
to take every detail down,
though I've imagined them
as they transform into rooks
and fly up, empty eyes looking past
empty steeples of stone churches.

Thank you, angels.
Thank you for looking away
as I bless my day from my own stone porch,
black dog at my side eyeing the squirrels,
and feel my own good ghost hovering near,
above my quiet morning self,
the one that shivers like mid-November air,
the one that can't stop staring
into the pine woods across the street
beyond the *No Trespassing* sign.

This morning I will bless our web of wind
for being unseen and for moving past.
I will bless that weft of crows
looking for anything to glean
from ground and branch
as line of wing crisscrosses
under white pines. I will bless
the maple branches lacing
upwards with nothing
but sky and crow between.
And next to me, I will bless
the blackness of my dog's fur,
the hunger for connection in his bark,
the look in his eyes that needs

to hear my voice, the teeth that would tear
to shreds my enemy's white wings.

IN A TIME OF DROUGHT, PRAISE

Let us praise this year without peaches,
praise these tomatoes, stunted,
half-ripened on the vine.

Let us praise the cucumber beetles,
who in two days will chew to lace
every leaf of the zucchini plant

I've watered daily for six weeks.
Let us praise all water and praise the insects
moving unseen beneath weeds,

who live to unbuild a garden's work,
bite by tiny bite, and thrive.
Let us praise all silent and unseen life.

Let us praise the two moths fluttering, stuck
on chicken wire, that I don't move to free,
and praise the sunflower's stalk drooping above,

head toppled, facing down.
Let me praise my own gloved hands
as they start tearing at dirt

around some kale to pull up weeds
by root, toss them in a pile to rot.
And let me praise my dog's black fur

soaking up the sun as he sleeps
on the other side of the fence.
Praise his heart and praise his lungs.

Praise his chest, the way it rises
and falls as he sleeps.
Praise his idle paws,

how they want both of us
to stay put late past midday heat,
devotion all around,

until our wingless backs
grow tired and knees ache
to rise above the ground.

THE HEART OF THE MATTER

As we walk by with our big black dog,
the neighbor boy sits cross-legged
on the cooling evening asphalt
of his driveway by the sugar maples,
beneath fluttering gypsy moths,
beneath the apple tree and oak branches
that wend their way above our street.
The boy's eyes look up, watching
for the nesting Cooper's Hawks
that've moved into the tree across the street.
Their eggs just hatched the other day
and when we've passed below we've often heard
hungry nestling chirps weaving air above us.
We stop and look up now, listening,
and hope that we might see a parent
swoop out and cross our field of vision,
wings extended and unmoving,
iron gaze piercing air for prey.

*

Storm warnings were issued earlier,
and clouds are moving in
but all air around us stills to silence.
Alert, our dog spies across the grass
a ground squirrel grown fat
in the full spring. Small eyes
dart from side to side
as the squirrel's muscles freeze.
The dog tugs at his leash,
wanting what he wants.

*

How much in balance it all seems—
a sliver of a moment in time
before a storm, pushing toward night,
thunder rumbling in the distance,
the dog not knowing why
he has to wait to go home,
three humans looking up
into the darkening heart
of evening air, eager for the silence
of a wide-winged feathered shadow
to float down out of the dimming
twisted branches of the oak
like a gray dream in last light
and snatch one life from a world
we'd like to think belongs to us.

UNSUNG SONG

Ambulance at the neighbor's house last night.
Lights flashed then ceased then stars got bright,

increased themselves without a word across the sky.
We still don't know what wasn't right.

No one's said a word to us since dawn.
Behind a fence, the neighbor's dog sleeps on their lawn

as if not one thing could go wrong.
Things dissolve in unsung parts of any song.

Poverty in a full bank account.
Insolvency after losses mount.

Shudder of compressor in a failing fridge.
Wind frequency that snaps a finished bridge.

A dog howling at a sound that we can't hear.
A neighbor's shouts next door, muffled but still clear.

POLICE LOG
    —*Concord, Massachusetts*

A drunken altercation in the woods
at Walden Pond. Unruly train passengers,
a verbal dispute with a wife, an intoxicated
man calling to say he has no reason to live,
a motion alarm activated, a black dog barking
for over thirty minutes, parking
complaints aplenty, in a backyard
a toy gun that looked like a real gun.

A border collie running away
from a golf cart, an aggressive fox,
an injured woodchuck on Plainfield Road,
a black lab lying in a cul-de-sac,
a small white cat running loose,
a raccoon on a back porch,
an injured deer that was not injured
but deceased.

A phone scam, bad checks passed,
windows smashed, paint splashed
on the brick wall of a school,
a broken latch on a storage shed
and spray-paint on the wall inside,
shots fired, permits expired,
a patient causing a disturbance
in an emergency room.

Landscapers starting leaf-blowers at dawn,
an annoying call from a telemarketer,
a black Toyota parked in a fire lane
at the hospital, an erratic operator swerving
and speeding, a minivan driving
aggressively, a white sedan smashing
through a wooden fence, a downed tree blocking
all access to a house.

A phone taken from an unlocked vehicle,
a license plate lost, a citation issued, a charge
of assault and battery brought, an arrest
on a default warrant, an unregistered
motor vehicle, a man operating
under the influence with an open container,
a license suspended for six months,
a summons to appear.

A neighbor who thinks a neighbor
may have a camera filming her property.
A neighbor who reports a neighbor
for sweeping leaves into the street.
A neighbor who reports a neighbor
for sleeping inside his car.
A neighbor complaining about the cars
of birdwatchers parked on the street.

A neighbor with a noise
complaint about a downstairs neighbor.
A woman complaining about a man
who won't stop calling her.
A son stealing money
from his mother for pot.
A wife calling to complain about a past incident
with her husband.

Suspicious activity on Bradford Street involving
two people in the back seat of a motor vehicle.
Suspicious activity on Lowell Road involving
a house sitter who found a sliding door open
and spilled cereal in the kitchen.
Suspicious activity by a woman wearing red
cowboy boots, who walked into First Parish,
screamed, and then left in a white car.

A gold bracelet with diamond inserts
found, a leather wallet lost, a silver motor vehicle
parked at St. Bernard's Cemetery, occupied
by a man with his head down. A woman
requesting assistance with a mouse on her stove.
A man with a broomstick
chasing wild turkeys down the road.
Two people with a black dog in Walden Woods
looking for a lost camera.

LOYAL COMPANIONS

My black dog chases a yellow ball across a field.
On a park bench not far away, a couple yields,

not looking at each other, phones in hands—
one face, lips moving, one face, gray as sand.

Wind picks up, blows old leaves past their feet,
clouds don't touch. Two pigeons want to eat,

circle near, blank eyes seeking scraps to take away,
to peck and scratch through hunger of another day.

A shoe kicks out and down and slaps the ground.
My dog returns, ball in mouth, and looks around.

Across an almost empty sky gray clouds unfurl.
The pigeons scatter upwards in a circling swirl—

flap of feather and shift of air as solid bodies rise,
outstretched wings flutter, inches from our eyes.

THE BEGINNING OF THE END OF THE BEGINNING

today turned fifty-five & not much
feels different except
some strength sapped &
many things seem to be going
who knows where
bits of memory headed
to that same vacant room
where you're not able
to remember any birthdays
or your childhood dog's name
or that your favorite food
is still pizza & where
more things ache
all the time until there's
a tingling a numbness
behind your eyes
that baffles & maddens
because nothing will ever be
the way it used to be
& anyway was never
the way it was
to begin with

ON THE MORNING OF A SUDDEN DEATH

You'll be given nothing obvious:
no sign you'll fail to see, or if you see,
fail to understand, or if you understand,
fail to take seriously—
no black cat yowling
beneath blossoming oaks,
no black dog stalking
the edges of your vision,
no urgent grackle-clatter
waking you when yesterday
you heard no birds at all.

Though maybe, waking,
your body will send some
slight signal soon forgot:
a tingle on tongue's tip,
a faint ringing in one ear,
a lingering numbness
in the fingertips, a pulsing
twitch behind the throat.

More likely: blue jays will screech
their hunger and mark the borders
of their day, a woodpecker will stutter
his beak against a rotting tree,
while all around, the ceaseless
cycling of the black-capped chickadee's
slurring two-toned call:
one note up, one note down,
one note up, one note down.

IN THIS OR ANY OTHER WORLD
    —because of C. K. Williams

My fourteen-year-old son has recently got into the habit
of pointing out to me—often in that tone of annoyed,
I-can't-believe-I-have-to-put-up-with-this-are-you-really-related-
    to-me
frustration that I remember I too took with my parents at
    his age—
some of my particular quirks and tics that have layered
    themselves onto my life
and merged and morphed and re-emerged in different shapes,
    just as
paint colors are layered and will peel away from the surfaces
    of clapboard houses.

Some of these things I was already at least vaguely aware of, like
my tendency to give our black dog endless new nicknames based
    on his quirks
or my habit of tilting my head to the left when looking someone
    in the eye
or forgetting to put my napkin on my lap at the dinner table
and instead fingering it nervously next to my plate,
or saying *melk* instead of *milk* or *pellow* for *pillow*
or always saying *Well... here we are. Home again, home again*
whenever we pull into the driveway, even if we've been gone
    only a short while.
But he's also mentioned things that I hadn't thought about—
my propensity for rubbing the ever-present three-day stubble on
    my chin
between my right thumb and forefinger when I'm trying
    to listen hard,
or absent-mindedly plucking hairs from my eyebrows when I'm
    feeling nervous.

And some of these things I'm now thinking about changing
because in truth I too find them a bit tiresome, though like any
    old dog

I'm not sure I'm capable of or can find the energy to change the
    tricks of behavior
that have soaked so deeply into the thick black fur of
    so many years
of my own thoughtless motion and speechless speech
and some of which I actually take some small measure
    of delight in
and that in truth are now a large part of who I am in the world
although I've always preferred to think that there's
    some me in me
beyond my simple sum of habit and routine and minor foibles.
    Maybe there is,
maybe there isn't, but even if I could change, I'm not sure I
    would, I think today,
as I watch cold April rain drip onto the leaves from last October
beneath the bare bush outside my window,
the leaves I never bothered raking away
beside the picket fence I never bothered painting
beside the bush I never bothered trimming—
because torpor is an easy road leading to habits
that can become so much of who you are as you roll slowly on,
creaking in to the outskirts of your final destination.

No, I don't think I'll change, because a time will soon come when,
even if he's diligent enough and wants to, my own son
probably won't be able to remember the sound of my voice
or the exact outline of my ears, and only the smallest particles
and clusters of image and speech will be available to his inner eye.
Maybe he'll think, *Is that all there was to him?* and there I'll be,
diluted in his memory to a collection of small motions
    of the head
or a tone of voice I used when talking to the dog,
the dust motes of my oddities floating nearly invisible through his
    daily life,
the verbal tics, the stock phrases and small anecdotes

that become minor legends in the retelling—
all of these small, annoying, but in their way joyful things
that, along with these words, he might recall
with a laugh and a shrug as he rubs his chin, looks his wife
        in the eye
and tilts his head at the dinner table, fingering his napkin,
his kids watching him with mild annoyance as their black dog
        sleeps on the rug—
as his life settles into all of what's left to him in this or
        any other world.

SOWING WINTER RYE

Overcast and cool November day
and our garden plot's plowed under.
My black dog barks
across the empty field behind.
I weigh heft of winter rye seed in my hand
and walk backwards,
back and forth across my plot.
A stream of seeds slides past each finger.
Back and forth, back and forth,
to set the soil for spring.
If I walk and sow this rye in fall,
then plant new seedlings on my knees in May,
this plot, though small and bounded,
might bear a summer bounty
of beans, of kale, of peppers,
tomatoes more than we can eat.

A red-tailed hawk eyes
a different story from an oak.
I'm almost sixty now.
My son's not here.
The dog's bark rises
through the weight of air,
and together with the hawk, heads
toward cumulonimbus clouds on high,
mottled gray and purple black,
massed in stacks across our sky.

PUGET SOUND

This morning at 5 o'clock, a steaming cup of coffee
cooling in front of me on the dining room table,
in New England, April snow falling through the silence
outside my window, I keep trying to write about life
in Seattle, where I was married for the second time,
where my son was born, squinting and wrinkled and crying
on a clear summer's day with the Mountain out,
where we had a house with a cat but no dog on the west side
of Queen Anne Hill overlooking Puget Sound,
where once it rained every day for 100 straight days,
where most of the time I think I was just this side of happy.

But I keep coming back to the people alone in their cars
who'd sit silent in parking lots next to the shore of the Sound
and wouldn't get out no matter the weather—
just sit and look westward, windows closed,
engines idling toward the distant horizon.
I'm still trying to understand why,
as I sit here with snow falling
and my wife asleep upstairs in the semi-dark
and my black dog sleeping on the carpet next to me,
icebox thrumming in the kitchen, son 2000 miles west of here,
a young man skiing the snowy Sawtooths.

I still can't make out the faces, lost behind windshield glass—
I only see wisps of car exhaust rising into morning haze
floating in off the water as I bike past on my way to work,
gulls shrieking over fish bones, horn-blast of a ferry rumbling
in my chest as the ship slips away from the dock, churning
west to Bainbridge, rough arc of foam fading in its wake,
sharp stone edges of Olympic peaks looking soft
on the other side of the Sound.

STILL LIFE, WITH MARRIAGE

We pass together through our street,
black dog at our side—smell of rose-bed mulch,
red flash of cardinal perched above
on a bare branch of the March apple tree.
On the other side, the brown of the female,
almost invisible, but still singing.

It's difficult to see wing-shifts, beak-lifts,
as bird-call works back and forth
in morning air, then floats away
from us, as it builds moment to moment
an only-moving, an always moving
trellis of connection.

We return home and feed the dog,
move into the business of another day,
the getting and the spending—
what we call work—loving and hating
our routines, this getting by,
but still feeling the echo
of how our day began—

tableau of birds in tree,
rose-bed mulch below,
hand touching hand,
dog sniffing a flower bed—
caught in one moment
against a backdrop
of unmoving sun,
earth not spinning
for a moment,
then morning sky thinning,
as we continued to walk
into the smooth turning
at the end of our street,

world in rhythm with our feet,
bird-song still above us
one note calling to another,
though we still can't tell
which to which.

NOTES

"On Being a Dog" was inspired by Ross Gay's "On Becoming a Horse."

"All Bark" was inspired by and is a response to lowellgm's "Not Birds."

"Police Log" was pieced together using rewritten and edited entries taken over a two-year period from the "Police Log" column in *The Concord* (Mass.) *Journal*.

WITH THANKS

I owe a considerable debt of gratitude to the friends and poets who read early versions of many of these poems and provided wise, insightful comments.

Boundless thanks are due to the amazingly supportive members of the weekly "Potts Poetry" group in Boston, who have provided me with so much encouragement and, more importantly, astute criticism, over the last ten years or so during our weekly workshops in the basement AGNI offices at Boston University: Amy M. Clark, Kirun Kapur, Michael Perrow, Lynne Potts, Lindsey O'Neill, Carla Panciera, Beth Woodcome Platow, Glenn Stowell, Kate Westhaver, Leslie Williams, and Scott Withiam. Potts Poets, where would I be without you all? Nowhere I'd want to be, that's where.

Many thanks as well to other readers—in particular William Allen, Maria Barthold-Bosch, and Christa Collins—who saw and commented on early versions of some of the poems included here.

As always, none of my poems would be possible without the support and love of my family: my son, Alex, and my incomparable wife, Christina. Every day I thank my lucky stars that you are both in my life.

Photographer, technical writer, bicycling aficionado, Nordic ski enthusiast, and dog lover, **Brian Burt** is the author of the poetry collection *Past Continuous* (2015), which was praised by critic Sven Birkerts as "redemptive" with poems "conveying their intelligence through clarity and the felt rightness of their every small decision." Burt's poems have appeared in a variety of print and online publications, including *The Independent, The Drum, FUSION, The Hiram Poetry Review,* and *The Spoon River Quarterly.* He is a recipient of the Michael R. Gutterman Award for Poetry and was a finalist for the New American Poetry Prize in 2012. His poems have also been featured on WGLT's (now defunct) "Poetry Radio" podcast and broadcast. He lives in Concord, Massachusetts, with his family plus two black cats and a big black dog.

www.ingramcontent.com/pod-product-compliance
Lightning Source LLC
LaVergne TN
LVHW041510070426
835507LV00012B/1473